Parliament at work

Derek Heater

Oxford

in association with the Hansard Society
for Parliamentary Government

F

Contents

21115186P

21115186P

TS

ned on or before

Oxford University Press, Walton Street, Oxford OX2 6DP

Oxford New York Toronto
Delhi Bombay Calcutta Madras Karachi
Petaling Jaya Singapore Hong Kong Tokyo
Nairobi Dar es Salaam Cape Town
Melbourne Auckland

and associated companies in
Berlin Ibadan

Oxford is a trademark of Oxford University Press

ISBN 0 19 832921 0

Typesetting by Burns & Smith, Derby
Printed and bound in Great Britain by
William Clowes Limited, Beccles and London

Acknowledgements

The publishers would like to thank the following for supplying
illustrations:
David Ace/The Observer, p.31; M. Cummings, p.41; Les
Gibbard/The Guardian, p.33; H.M.S.O., p.11; Popperfoto,
p.4; The Press Association, p.9 and p.27; Punch, p.30 and p.39.
Additional illustrations by Ray Fishwick, Gecko Limited, John
Ireland, Sharon Pallent, Julia Quenzler.

Cover photograph by Adam Woolfitt/Susan Griggs Agency Ltd

1
The Palace of Westminster

Origins of the building

The British people love tradition and do not like to discard old habits. Yet this regard for the past can have unforeseen consequences. So it was with the old Palace of Westminster. Here, over the centuries a huge store of tallies had accumulated—medieval government accounts kept on notched wooden sticks. It suddenly occurred to someone in 1834 that they were not exactly useful—except as firewood. A zealous stoker heaped them in to the House of Lords stove, which became overheated. Wooden panels caught alight. Within a few hours only Westminster Hall and the Cloisters were left standing beside the charred ruins.

The present building was designed by Charles Barry. Its design disappointed many people at the time. One critic, commenting on its numerous pinnacles, said it looked like an upturned sow! Nevertheless, it soon grew in the nation's affections.

Big Ben

Probably the most famous part of the building is the Clock Tower. This houses Big Ben, the clock bell named after Sir Benjamin Hall, who was responsible for its installation. The dials of the clock, 23 feet in diameter, have appeared in countless photographs and films. The chimes are regularly broadcast by B.B.C. radio. The full hour change, with the traditional words is as follows:

Lord through this hour, Be thou our guide,

That by Thy power, No foot shall slide.

The Houses of Parliament
Plan of the Principal Floor

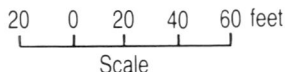

1 St Stephen's Entrance
Visitors to the Palace of Westminster must use this entrance. Because of the fear of terrorist attack a special security point has been built just inside. Members of Parliament and Peers have their separate entrances, which are shown on the diagram.

3 St Stephen's Hall
Leading straight on from the entrance is St Stephen's Hall, the site of the Commons' chamber until the fire of 1834. This is a particularly fascinating area for the visitor. Here may be seen the spot where Spencer Perceval was shot in 1812—the only British prime minister to have been assassinated. Also statues of famous seventeenth and eighteenth parliamentarians are here; and murals depicting various episodes from English history.

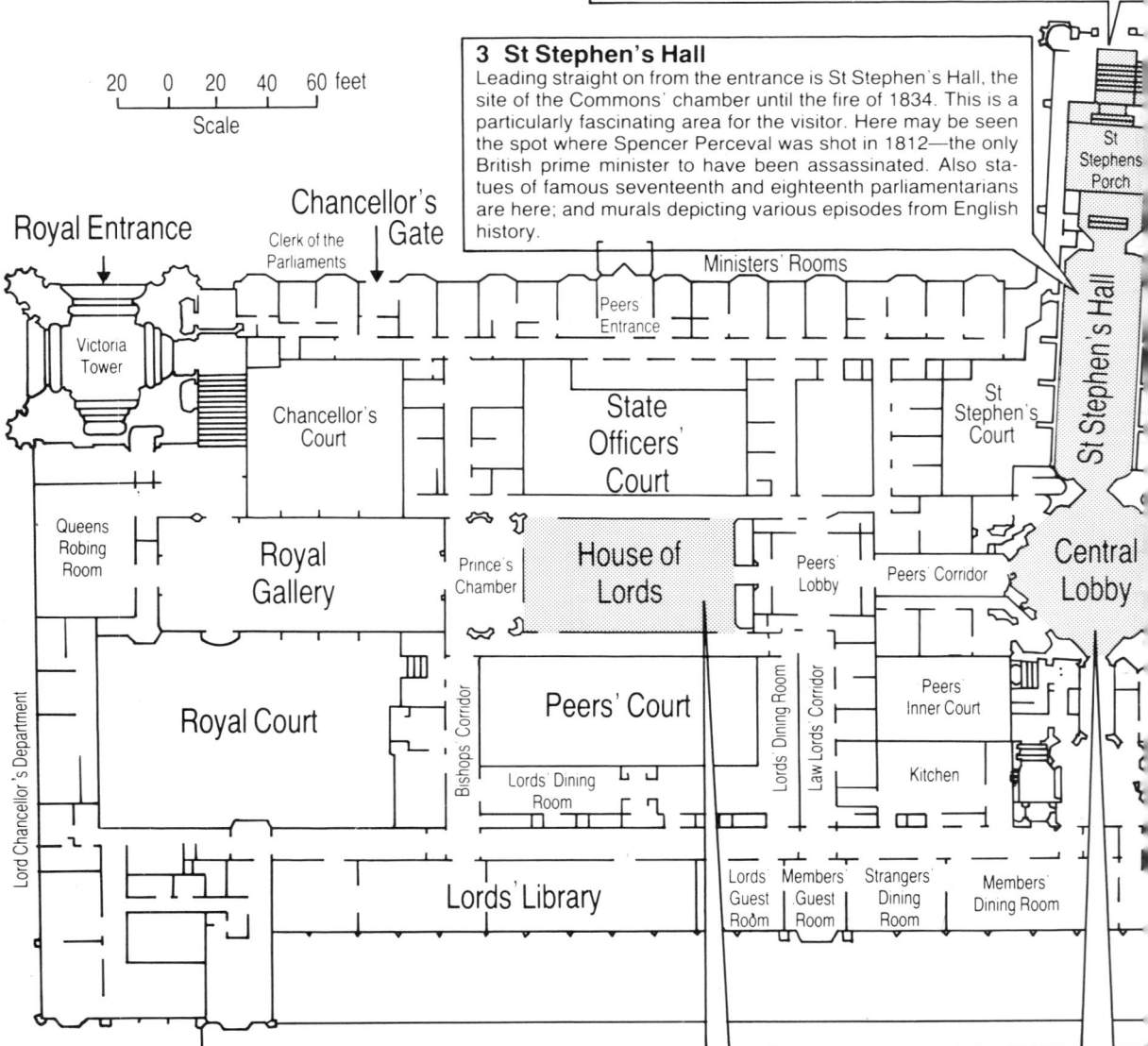

```
20   0   20   40   60 feet
|_____|____|____|____|
        Scale
```

Royal Entrance

Chancellor's Gate

Clerk of the Parliaments

Ministers' Rooms

Peers Entrance

St Stephens Porch

Victoria Tower

Chancellor's Court

State Officers' Court

St Stephen's Court

St Stephen's Hall

Queens Robing Room

Royal Gallery

Prince's Chamber

House of Lords

Peers' Lobby

Peers' Corridor

Central Lobby

Lord Chancellor's Department

Royal Court

Bishops' Corridor

Peers' Court

Lords' Dining Room

Law Lords Corridor

Peers' Inner Court

Kitchen

Lords' Dining Room

Lords' Library

Lords Guest Room

Members' Guest Room

Strangers' Dining Room

Members' Dining Room

5 The House of Lords
The corridor to the south or right of the Central Lobby leads to the House of Lords. At the far end stands the royal throne used during the State Opening of Parliament. In front of these is the Lord Chancellor's Woolsack.

4 Central Lobby
St. Stephen's Hall leads to the Central Lobby, where, for example, constituents may meet their M.P. More statues may be seen here, including that of Gladstone.

2 Westminster Hall

Immediately to the left of the security booth, stone steps descend to Westminster Hall, built nearly 900 years ago in the reign of William Rufus, though slightly changed three hundred years later. It is used occasionally for important and grand ceremonies.

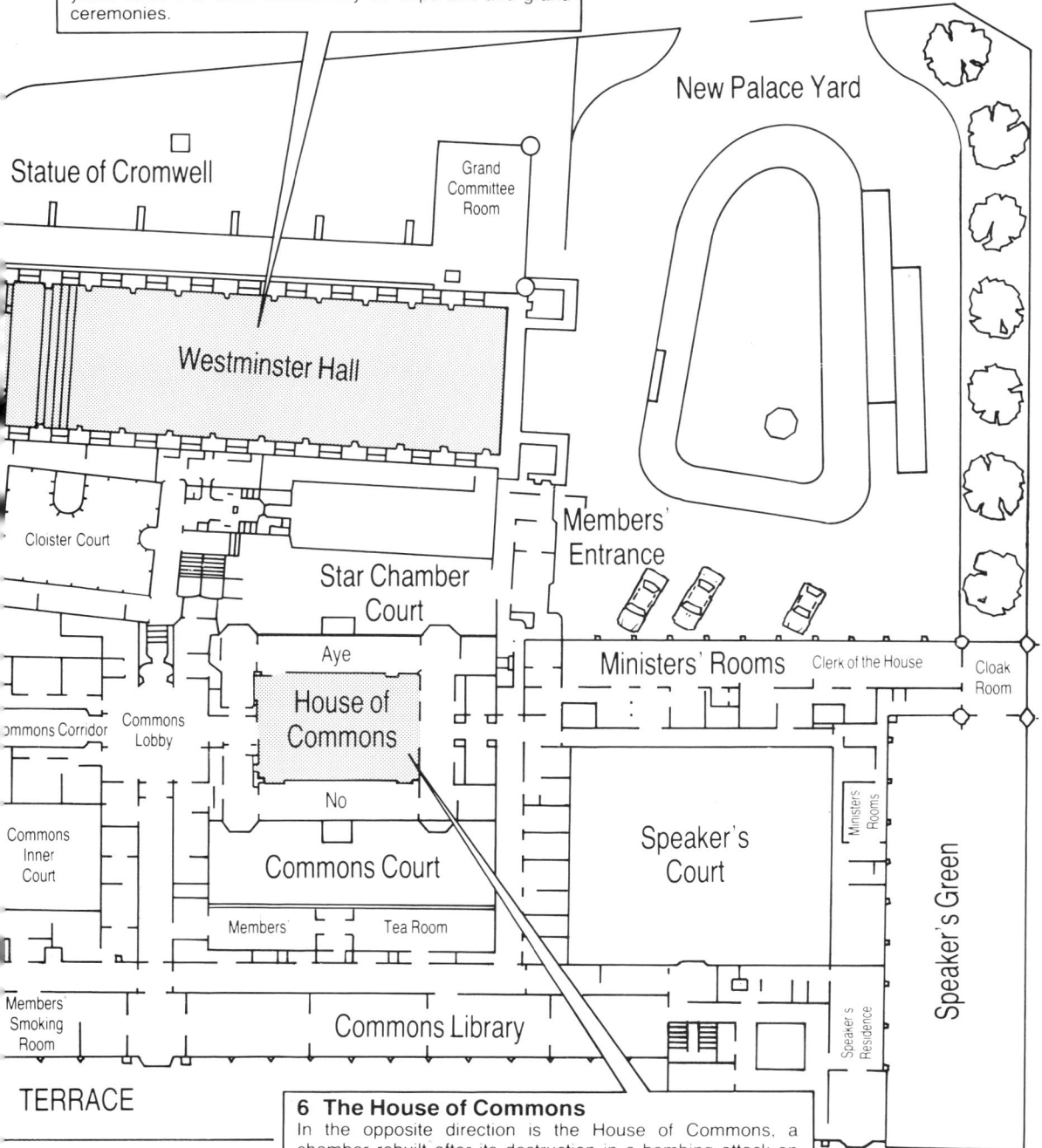

New Palace Yard

Statue of Cromwell

Grand Committee Room

Westminster Hall

Cloister Court

Members' Entrance

Star Chamber Court

Aye

Ministers' Rooms

Clerk of the House

Cloak Room

ommons Corridor

Commons Lobby

House of Commons

No

Speaker's Court

Ministers Rooms

Speaker's Green

Commons Inner Court

Commons Court

Members

Tea Room

Members' Smoking Room

Commons Library

Speaker's Residence

TERRACE

6 The House of Commons

In the opposite direction is the House of Commons, a chamber rebuilt after its destruction in a bombing attack on the building during the Second World War. At one end is the Speaker's chair. To the right of the Speaker are the Government benches, behind which is the 'Aye' voting lobby. To the left are the Opposition benches and the 'No' lobby. Immediately in front of the Speaker and between the 'front benches' of the Government and Opposition leaders is the table. Here sit the clerks and here is placed the Speaker's Mace when the House is in session.

Other rooms

The plan shows you the other rooms on the ground floor. On the first floor are rows of committee rooms—hence the term to take a Bill 'upstairs' when it reaches the committee stage (see p.20). The committee rooms are used for a wide variety of meetings, including those involving private citizens as well as M.P.s and peers.

The Palace of Westminster is now too small to cope with all the needs of Parliament so that some M.P.s and staff have rooms for their work and secretaries in a nearby building.

The chamber of the House of Commons

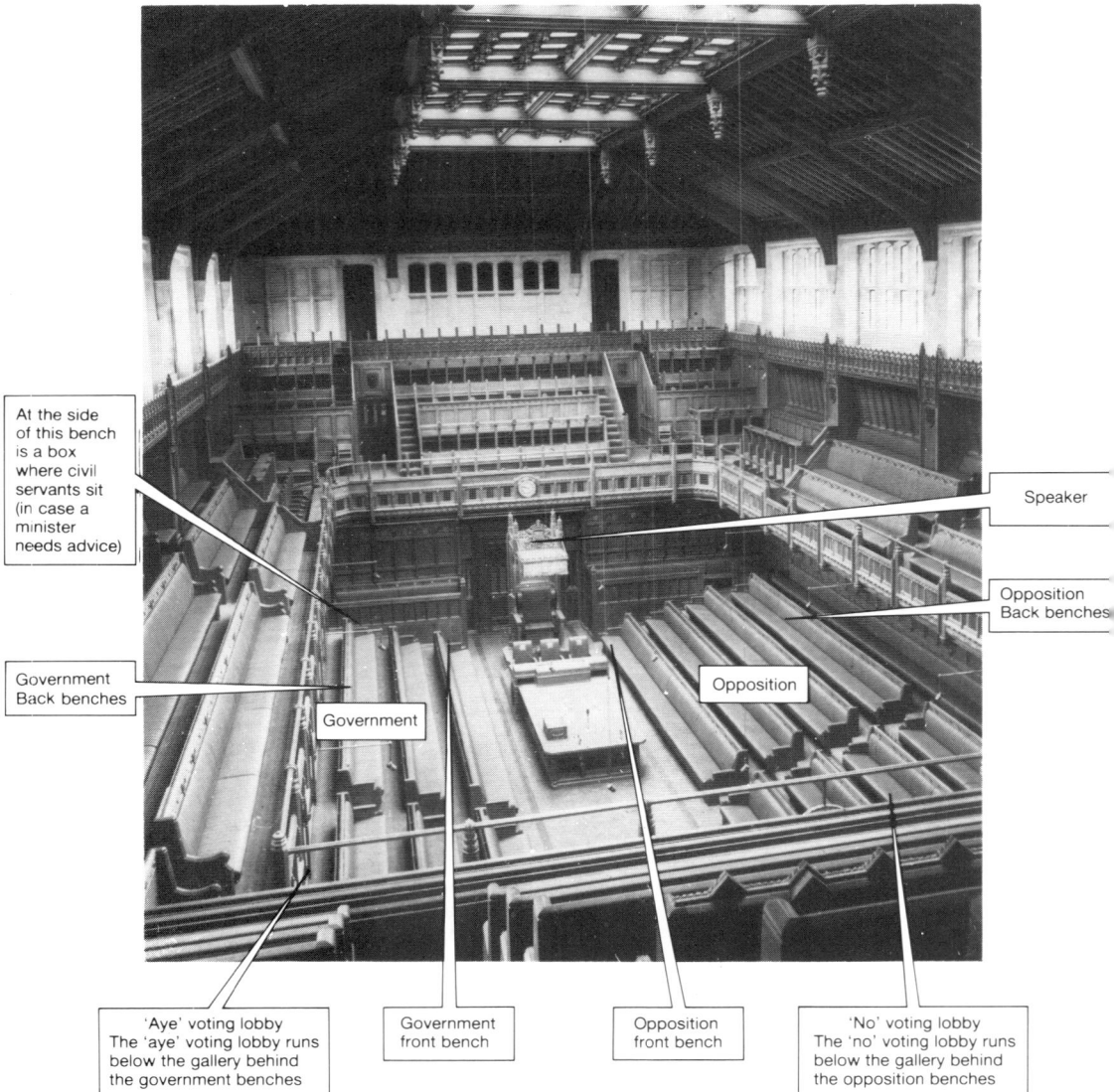

At the side of this bench is a box where civil servants sit (in case a minister needs advice)

Speaker

Opposition Back benches

Government Back benches

Opposition

Government

Government front bench

Opposition front bench

'Aye' voting lobby
The 'aye' voting lobby runs below the gallery behind the government benches

'No' voting lobby
The 'no' voting lobby runs below the gallery behind the opposition benches

2
Parliamentary officers and officials

The Speaker of the House of Commons

Mr Speaker's role

When, at 2.00 p.m., the Speaker's procession wends its dignified way from the Speaker's House to the Chamber of the House of Commons all present stand in respect. While presiding over debates the Speaker may be heard above the excitment or anger of political controversy commanding 'Order! Order!' These contrasting scenes represent perhaps the extent of many people's knowledge of the role of Speaker of the House of Commons. These two aspects of his duties do indeed reveal much about the general character of the office: tradition and authority. For, to define his function merely as chairman of the House of Commons is to miss much of the richness of his job.

Ceremony and tradition

The evolution of his role can be traced back to the fourteenth century, when it was found to be necessary to have one man as a channel of communication between the Commons and the King. Over the centuries the prime loyalty of the Speaker gradually shifted from the Monarch to Parliament. The Speaker remains the formal representative of the House of Commons outside the Palace of Westminster. The symbol of his authority is the Mace, lent to the House by the Queen and carried in the procession by the Serjeant at Arms (see p.7). It is placed on the Table in front of the Speaker when the Commons is in session to show that he or his deputy is presiding.

Authority

The Speaker's life is a lonely one. He lives in rooms in the Palace of Westminster overlooking the Thames. And from being a politically committed M.P. (Speakers are chosen from among their ranks, of course), he must become completely impartial. No more chats in political clubs. He must even be careful about his social life in the House of Commons, 'the best club in London', in the words of Dickens. He must be a person with a rare mix of qualities: he has to be able to cope without the company of his fellow M.P.s; be respected for his impartiality; possess a sound knowledge of parliamentary procedure; be endowed with tact and judgment in handling debates; and have a firmness of command in controlling the House.

Some of the main functions of the Speaker are as follow:
1. He conducts debates by calling upon M.P.s, who can speak only when they 'catch the Speaker's eye'.
2. He disciplines M.P.s for unruliness. He can 'name' such individuals and have them excluded from the proceedings.
3. He decides how many supplementary questions may be asked at Question Time.
4. He decides whether a closure motion should be accepted.
5. He supervises the voting in divisions.
6. He selects chairmen of standing committees (see p.20).
7. He decides whether a complaint of a breach of parliamentary privilege should be given precedence for debate in the House.

A problem

Mr Speaker remains an M.P. He is chosen on his merits, irrespective of party. But when he takes up his office, his constituency is affected in two ways: by his surrender of party allegiance; and because of the time-consuming nature of his job, he may have to nominate an M.P. from a neighbouring constituency to look after some of its affairs.

Lord Chancellor

Mr Speaker's opposite number as 'chairman' of the House of Lords is the Lord Chancellor, who presides, with equal respect for tradition, from the Woolsack, symbol of the source of medieval England's prosperity. His task is less formalised than the Speaker's since the conduct of business in the Upper House is less strictly regulated. For example, the Lord Chancellor is not responsible for maintaining order (but then bishops, lords and ladies tend to behave themselves with so much greater restraint than M.P.s!) and has no powers to regulate debate. Because his task is lighter, the Lord Chancellor also has time to perform the function of head of the English judiciary. He is also a member of the Cabinet. Consequently he is a member simultaneously of all three branches of the constitution: legislative, judiciary and executive—a nightmare situation for supporters, like the Americans, of the principle of the separation of powers.

The Serjeant at Arms

As Mace-bearer and 'bouncer' for coping with unruly 'named' M.P.s, Mr Speaker has the services of a Royal Court official, the Serjeant at Arms. But these are not the only duties of the Serjeant at Arms' department, which is also responsible for general security and office services.

Black Rod

A similar function is performed for
the House of Lords by the
Gentleman Usher of the Black Rod.
It is he who formally summons the
Commons to attend upon the
Monarch in the House of Lords on
the occasion of the State Opening of
Parliament.

The Clerks

The conduct of parliamentary business and the keeping of records
must of course conform to clear rules and standards of accuracy.
Both Houses have Departments of Clerks to advise members on
procedure and ensure the smooth running of affairs in this regard.
The head of the Lord's team is called 'the Clerk of the Parliaments',
and of the Commons', 'the Clerk of the House of Commons'.

Other Departments of the House of Commons

To keep a large institution like the House of Commons running
efficiently obviously requires an Administration Department,
which deals with pay, allowances and other financial matters and
with staffing questions.

The House of Commons Library provides M.P.s with books and
newspapers and with the reference and research facilities including
statistical data, necessary for the effective discharge of their duties.

There is also the Department of the Offical Report (or *Hansard*),
which reports the debates of the House and of many committees.
Its reports are published daily while the House is in session.

Finally, essential services are provided for over 2000 Members
and staff by the Refreshment Department, in a number of dining
rooms, cafeterias and bars. There are similar departments in the
House of Lords.

The Ombudsman

In understanding the mechanics of Parliament we must not, however, lose sight of the fact that it exists to look after the interests of the people as a whole. And in recent years it has become obvious that ordinary people sometimes need protection from bad and unjust decisions taken by civil servants. Consequently in 1967 a new official was appointed, the Parliamentary Commissioner for Administration. Any M.P. can request on behalf of a constituent that he investigate a complaint—though he has no power to over-turn any miscarriage of justice or to enforce compensation for the grievance. Nevertheless, ministers do act on his recommendations.

The title of the Parliamentary Commissioner is rather cumber-some. He is usually referred to as the Ombudsman, a Scandinavian word, for it was in those countries that the system was first introduced. He also investigates complaints regarding the National Health Service.

The procession from the Commons to the Lords at the State Opening of Parliament

3
The daily routine

The need for rules

Many debating societies conduct their discussions in ways very similar to the House of Commons. After all, the House of Commons is the most important debating society in the land. It is, however, more than that—it is a major component of the governmental system of a complex, industrialised society. It is obvious, therefore, that very clear rules of procedure must be available and adhered to. Many of these are embodied in Standing Orders.

The basic principles are that the Government should be given generous opportunity to conduct its business and therefore the major allocation of time; all interests should also nevertheless be allowed to express their views; a clear agenda of business must be published; and rules of courtesy should prevail for orderly debate.

The time table of business

The basic pattern

The main business in the chamber is normally undertaken from 2.30 to 10.30 p.m. on Mondays to Thursdays and from 9.30 a.m. to 3.0 p.m. on Fridays (to allow M.P.s to return to their constituencies on Friday evenings). Other business, however, delays the rising of the House, on most days, to about midnight. Apart from sundry business the 'day' starts with nearly an hour of Question Time (except on Fridays) (see p.24), while the bulk of time is devoted to Government business, and occasionally Opposition motions (see p.18) and private Members motions and bills.

Arrangements 'behind the Speaker's chair'

So that the proceedings may run as smoothly as possible discussions take place unofficially between the parties (hence the term 'behind the Speaker's chair') to map out and agree the agenda for the following week. In this way party leaders and Whips can try to ensure that the allocation of the time is as productive as possible and to avoid procedural wrangles on the floor of the House. The programme for the following week is then announced by the Leader of the House each Thursday. In addition, the names of those due to be the major speakers and any M.P.s wishing to contribute will be made known to the Speaker.

Two brief words of explanation are needed here. 'Whips' are the 'prefects', who ensure that the members of their parties attend and vote at crucial times. The Leader of the House is the member of the Cabinet responsible for ensuring the smooth passage of Government business through the Commons.

Order Papers

Each day's business is printed as a kind of pamphlet known as the Order Paper. Only in exceptional circumstances will the Speaker allow the House to be diverted from this agenda.

Extracts from an Order Paper

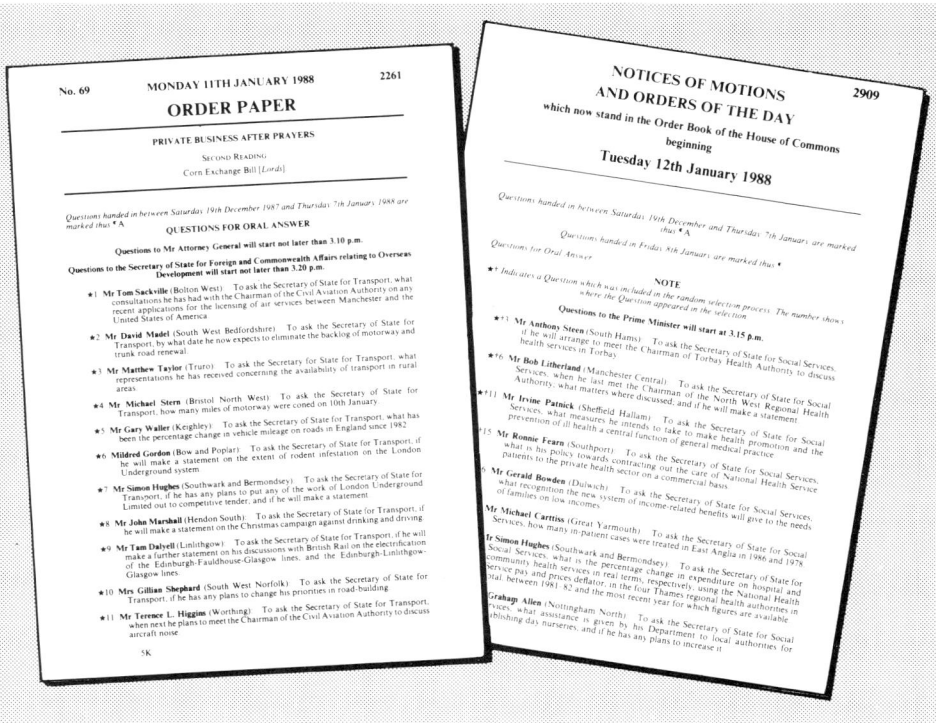

Rules of debate

The various kinds of debate are outlined in Chapter 8. It is important to note here that a number of devices exist in an attempt to foster an atmosphere of decorum. An M.P. must stand when speaking. He must address the Speaker. He must refer to fellow members by their appropriate titles (e.g. the hon. Member for Blanksville South).

And no member, on pain of disciplinary action by the Speaker, may use 'unparliamentary language'. A member may have good reason to believe that another has lied or been a scoundrel but neither of those words may be uttered. There are many diverting anecdotes relating to this issue. My favourite concerns Disraeli, who once asserted, 'Half the Cabinet are asses.' He was required to withdraw this remark. He readily did so, amending it to, 'Half the Cabinet are not asses.' (The Speaker would not disallow such a comment today — fashions change.)

Ways of concluding business

Simple closure

Unless a debate ends naturally, because no one else seeks to speak, a decision may have to be made to bring it to an end. This is normally undertaken by the regulation in Standing Order No. 35. An M.P. (often a Government Whip) moves that 'the question be now put'. If the Speaker considers this reasonable, and a substantial majority of the House agree, the debate is concluded and the vote is taken.

The 'guillotine'

In order to speed up business the Government sometimes secures the agreement of the House for a specific allocation of time for debating each section of a bill. Thus, however anxious the Opposition may be to continue argument, the debate is 'chopped off' (hence the rather gruesome term 'guillotine') when the time has been exhausted.

Voting

When the House 'divides' in order to count the numbers for and against a motion, the M.P.s leave the chamber and are counted by 'tellers' as they pass through their chosen lobby— 'ayes' and 'noes'. Their names are recorded by the Clerks.

Hansard

A full record of parliamentary debates is very important: as evidence for historians, for reference by politicians, and as information for ordinary citizens. Nevertheless, it was not until the nineteenth century that Parliament conceded that it was not a breach of privilege for its proceedings to be published. Even as late as 1771 the Lord Mayor of London was incarcerated in the Tower for daring to be involved in such reporting. In the nineteenth century a family of publishers by the name of Hansard undertook the printing — hence the name. The reporting was a private venture at first and not until 1909 did *Hansard* become an official publication in its present form.

Today both Commons and Lords have their *Hansards*. Everything that is said in each of the two chambers is printed; and nothing may be changed or added. And so however small the attendance might be to hear a speech, it is always available to be read.

4
Members of
Parliament

The number of M.P.s

Every ten to fifteen years the boundary commissioners set to work. These are groups of impartial people, chaired by the Speaker, to decide exactly where the boundaries of constituencies should be drawn. After all, the principle of 'one person, one vote' would not mean very much if some M.P.s were elected by a tiny electorate and others by a huge. In the 1987 election 650 M.P.s were elected, representing on average about 70,000 people. These were divided among the parties as follows:

Conservatives	375	Scottish and/Welsh	
Labour	229	Nationalist	6
Liberal/SDP Alliance	22	Ulster parties	18

How M.P.s are selected

Although you can vote if you are 18, you cannot be an M.P. unless you are 21. Nor can you be an M.P. if you have certain jobs (for example, policeman, a judge, a civil servant), or you are an Anglican or Roman Catholic clergyman, an undischarged bankrupt, a prisoner serving a sentence of a year or more, a lunatic or a peer (member of the House of Lords). Apart from individual candidates some of whom stand for frivolous reasons, the great majority are selected by organised political parties. Usually a candidate is chosen by a small group of party workers in the constituency, though subject to some control from national headquarters.

The issue of selection has in recent years become very controversial in the Labour Party. Some constituency organisations became dominated by Militants, whose revolutionary left-wing views were not shared by the Party leaders. Also, left-wingers introduced the right of reselection: that is, an established candidate or even a sitting M.P. would not automatically be chosen as the candidate in a subsequent election.

The way parties select their candidates is, of course, crucial. Voters can only vote for individuals who have already overcome this initial hurdle.

Who are our M.P.s?

Background

A survey of age and educational and professional background of M.P.s in the mid-1980s gives some idea of the kind of individuals who become the people's representatives. Just under one-sixth were over 60, while just under one-sixtieth were under 30. About two-thirds had attended university. By far and away the largest professional groups were company directors and lawyers, accounting together for well over a third of the members of the House.

How representative are our representatives?

M.P.s are often criticised for being mere publicity-seekers, quite unlike the citizens they represent and therefore out-of-touch with the interests and needs of the country. In the famous television series, *Yes, Minister*, for example, the main character, Jim Hacker once said, 'Being an M.P. is a vast subsidised ego trip. It is a job which needs no qualifications ... and provides a warm room and subsidised meals to a bunch of self-opinionated windbags and busy bodies.'

In a sense M.Ps. should not be the same as their constituents. M.Ps. need to be above the average in intelligence, fluency, knowledge, conscientiousness and energy. And almost all are, despite Hacker's little quip.

What is perhaps rather worrying is that so few working-class, black and female M.Ps. are elected. In 1987 the largest-ever numbers of black (4) and women (41) M.Ps. were returned.

1987

Afro-Asian MP's   Women MP's

Pay and facilities

The payment of M.Ps. is a tricky problem. If they are paid too little, only people with private means could afford to become M.Ps. If they are paid too much, undesirable people may become members merely for the sake of the money. The salary level is now linked to that of middle-grade civil servants (subject to periodic review by the Plowden Review Body on Top Salaries).

In 1987 the salary of ordinary M.Ps. (ministers are paid more) was £22,500 p.a. In addition they receive a number of allowances related to their work. These include: free travel on parliamentary business within the U.K.; a sum for research and secretarial assistance; and overnight subsistence for time spent in London.

Compared with representatives in other 'Western' countries British M.Ps. are not generously treated. Considering that many find it necessary to have two places to live (in their constituency and in London) their pay is modest. Office accommodation and research/secretarial assistance must often be shared. Furthermore, since they average a 67-hour week (according to a recent survey), often in unsocial hours, many M.Ps. feel that their conditions of work could, in the interests of fairness and efficiency, be improved.

The June 1987 election results for London (*below*) show a pattern that is typical for the country as a whole, with Labour winning most of the inner city seats and the Conservatives winning in the suburbs. This shows up on the inset map of Britain, which also shows that Scotland and Wales were predominantly Labour too, although here many of the rural constituencies were won by non-Labour opposition parties.

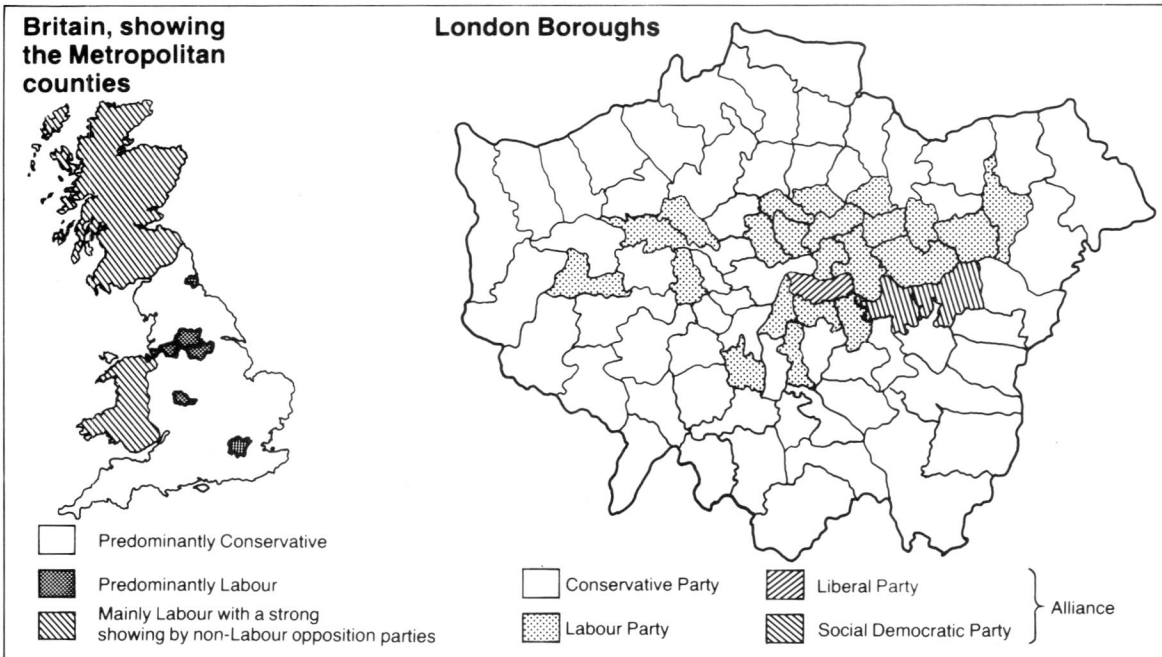

Britain, showing the Metropolitan counties

London Boroughs

☐ Predominantly Conservative

▨ Predominantly Labour

▨ Mainly Labour with a strong showing by non-Labour opposition parties

☐ Conservative Party

▨ Labour Party

▨ Liberal Party

▨ Social Democratic Party

} Alliance

5
Legislation

Different kinds of legislation

The role of Parliament

There are basically three ways of making laws. First, one person (a king or a dictator) or a small group (an oligarchy or a military *junta*) can issue decrees. Secondly, all the citizens can gather together and vote as they did during the democratic era in ancient Athens. Thirdly, the elected representatives of the people can decide. The first system allows no freedom; the second is impractical in large modern states. Britain is, generally speaking, served well by a system in which elected representatives (the House of Commons) are responsible for most of the nation's legislation.

A proposal to change the law is called a Bill. When it has been fully scrutinised and approved in the ways described below it becomes an Act of Parliament, a Statute. Most are Public Bills. These can be introduced by the Government or by Private Members. Others are Private Bills. Together, around one hundred are passed each year.

Government Bills

Of the different kinds of public Bills the majority that are passed into law are Government Bills. Also, very few of the Bills introduced by the Government are in practice rejected by Parliament. The reasons for this are partly the way the Government can control Parliament and partly the amount of preparatory work undertaken before the Bill is presented in any case. Interest groups are consulted; sometimes a Green Paper is produced, inviting comments, or a White Paper, outlining the proposals; the Bill is carefully drafted by lawyers; and it is discussed in Cabinet.

Private Members' Bills

Any M.P. or peer may introduce a Bill which he or she thinks would improve the law for the nation as a whole. Only a minority of these Bills are passed in practice, mainly because of inadequate time for dealing with them.

Private Bills

These relate not to the country as a whole but to bodies such as a particular local authority, private company or nationalised industry.

Secondary legislation

There are coming into force in Britain an increasing number of laws which are not necessarily approved by Parliament. However, Parliament has Committees to examine these. One kind is called delegated legislation. This means that Ministers have the power specifically given them by Act in some circumstances to change the law without introducing a Bill (subject to some degree of Parliamentary sanction).

The other kind of legislation comes from the European Commission. We shall see on p.23 that Britain must accept laws produced by the European Community as a whole. So that the U.K. Parliament can suggest amendments, each of the two Houses has a Select Committee on European legislation. The House of Lords' European Communities Committee looks at selected proposals more thoroughly than the Commons'; the European Legislation Committee looks at all proposals submitted to the Council of Ministers, but in less detail.

From Bill to Act

General principles

All Public Bills must pass through five required stages of scrutiny in both Houses before they can become law. Most Bills begin in the Commons, so let us trace the progress of a Bill from this starting-point.

The Stages

1. **First reading**. This is just the formal introduction of the Bill.

2. **Second Reading**. The House debates the general principles of the Bill to decide whether it should be allowed to proceed to detailed consideration.

3. **Committee Stage**. The whole Bill is examined in detail, clause by clause, by a committee. Usually this is a small Standing Committee (see p.20). Very occasionally, however, a Select Committee is used (see p.21); and sometimes all the M.Ps. undertake the task as a Committee of the Whole House. It is at this stage that amendments can be moved.

4. **Report Stage**. The House considers the Bill as amended after the Committee Stage, and more amendments are moved.

5. **Third Reading**. The Bill is debated in order to approve it (as amended). If it is approved, it is sent to the House of Lords. After the Lords have undertaken their task, they may make amendments, which the Commons and the Government (if it is a Government Bill) must decide how to handle—that is, to accept, reject or negotiate.

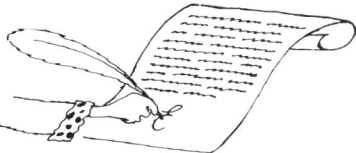

6. **Royal Assent**. Once the Bill has been accepted in exactly the same terms in each House it passes to the Queen for the formality of the Royal Assent. (Royal Assent has not been refused since 1707.)

6
The Parliament
Committee systems

The reasons for committees

Although the formal debating business of the House of Commons is confined to afternoons and evenings (and sometimes all through the night), it must not be thought that this is the only work M.Ps. undertake. Many engage in the tasks of the various Committees. It is fairly obvious that very detailed work such as examining the legal language of a Bill cannot be carried out by 650 M.Ps. crowded into a debating chamber. Hence the appointment of relatively small Committees—different kinds for different tasks.

Standing committees

We have seen in Chapter 5 that after its Second Reading a Bill is sent to a Committee. A separate Standing Committee is appointed to examine most Bills. The term 'Standing Committee' is very confusing because it usually means 'permanent'. However, these Committees are obviously temporary, being disbanded once their work on the Bill has been completed. The size ranges from 16 to 50 (usually about 20) and the members are chosen by party in proportion to the party membership of the House as a whole. Since most of the Bills come from the Government and that party will have a majority on each Committee, it is rare for Standing Committees to make major alterations.

In addition, Scottish and Welsh Grand Committees deal with the affairs of special concern to these parts of the United Kingdom. They are composed mainly of the Scottish and Welsh M.Ps. respectively.

Select Committees

Origins

The House is not only concerned with legislation. It is also concerned with oversight of Government policy and administration. One fairly obvious device for enabling the House of Commons to keep a watchful eye on the Government is a series of specialist Committees. And yet the idea was put into practice in a halting and haphazard way.

In 1861 Gladstone, when he was Chancellor of the Exchequer, arranged for the establishment of the Public Accounts Committee. It still exists, though over the years it has increased the range of its work to include a wide area of public expenditure to ensure that money is spent efficiently and wisely. Its chairman is always a member of the Opposition.

An Estimates Committee was set up after the 1939–45 war, and several other Committees were set up in the late 1960s and early 1970s because there was so much criticism of the failure of the House of Commons to keep an effective check on the Government. In 1979 a comprehensive array of fourteen new Select Committees (one for each main Government ministry or department) came into operation.

Departmental Select Committees

The following is the list of these Committees:
Agriculture; Defence; Education, Science and Arts; Employment; Energy; Environment; Foreign Affairs; Home Affairs; Industry and Trade; Scottish Affairs; Social Services; Transport; Treasury and Civil Service; Welsh Affairs.
The maximum size of each Committee is 11 (13 for Scottish Affairs) and each is composed of backbench M.Ps. Although the Government always has a majority of members, some chairmen are selected from the Opposition. The Committees have wide-ranging powers to consult specialist advisers, to examine papers and question ministers, civil servants and many outside bodies and individuals. They can also travel to see how things are being done in the U.K. or other countries.

But has the new Select Committee system been successful? It has certainly enabled a number of M.Ps. to become involved in checking the activities of the Government in some detail. Furthermore, some of the reports drawn up by the Committees are summarised in the news media so that the ordinary citizen can be better informed about these matters. The government might therefore be embarrassed by criticisms publicised in this way. On the other hand, there is nothing in the system which requires the Government to change its course of action.

There are also other Select Committees including—

1. Committees for running the House of Commons, dealing with such matters as catering, accommodation, procedure and Parliamentary Privilege.
2. Ad hoc Committees to cope with any unexpected matter needing investigation and a decision.
3. Secondary legislation (see p.18).

The different kinds of Parliamentary committee

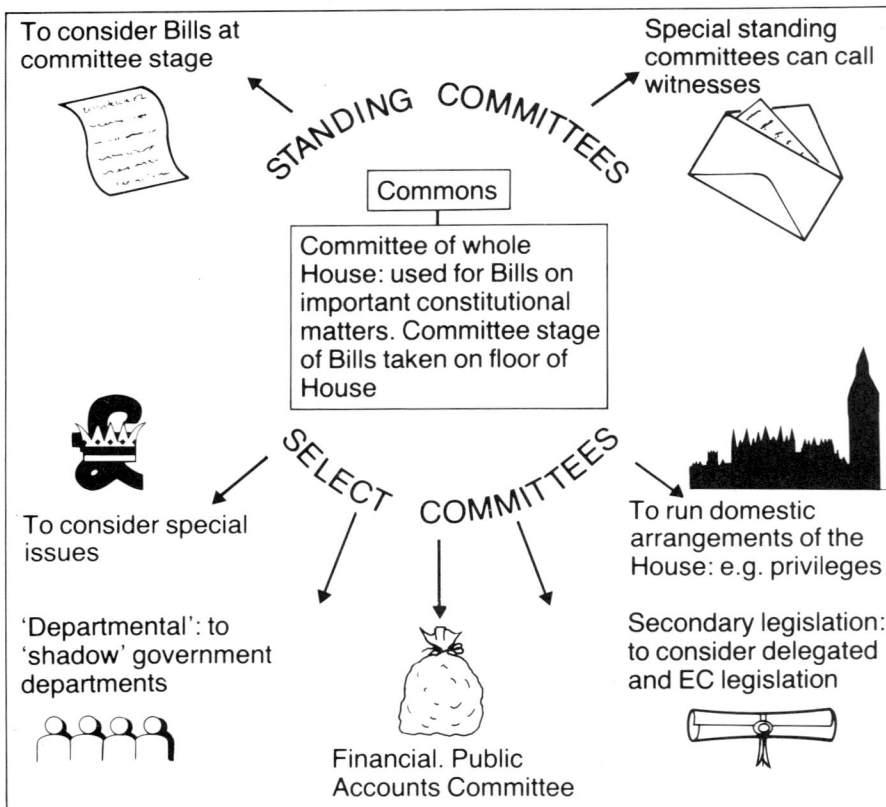

To consider Bills at committee stage

Special standing committees can call witnesses

STANDING COMMITTEES

Commons

Committee of whole House: used for Bills on important constitutional matters. Committee stage of Bills taken on floor of House

SELECT COMMITTEES

To consider special issues

'Departmental': to 'shadow' government departments

Financial. Public Accounts Committee

To run domestic arrangements of the House: e.g. privileges

Secondary legislation: to consider delegated and EC legislation

7
The powers of Parliament

Parliamentary sovereignty

In theory

Although Great Britain, unlike almost all other countries, has no written constitution, there is a wide measure of agreement that parliament holds the sovereign power in the land. Again, this constitutional theory sets Britain apart from many other states where sovereignty rests with the people and no single institution has such ultimate authority. The great constitutional theorist, A.V. Dicey, wrote almost exactly one hundred years ago that Parliament has 'the right to make or unmake any law whatever ...[and] no person or body is recognised by the law of England as having the right to override or set aside the legislation of Parliament.'

In practice

This theory means that no court of law, for example, can declare any decision made by Parliament to be illegal.

On the other hand, there are many ways in which the theoretical legal authority of Parliament is constrained in practice (although with the concurrence of Parliament). The most important recent example derives from Britain's membership of the European Community. When Britain joined in 1973 many M.Ps. expressed concern that the sovereignty of Parliament would necessarily be eroded. For the Treaty of Accession specifically provides for European Community law to override English law in the event of a conflict, whether Parliament likes it or not.

And in practice, Parliament legislature is controlled by the executive by the exercise of its majority in the Commons.

Accountability of the executive

General principles

One of the most important requirements of Parliament is that it should be alert—to be constantly scrutinising and questioning what the Government (that is, Ministers and Civil Servants) are doing. There are various devices for practising this vigilance: for example, Select Committees (see p.21); Debates (see p.28); and Question Time.

Question Time

2.35 to 3.30 p.m. Mondays to Thursdays is the time set aside as Parliamentary Question (PQ) Time. Thus for a few hours a week Ministers (including the Prime Minister on Tuesdays and Thursdays, 3.15 to 3.30) are required to give information and defend the actions of their departments.

   The procedure is for M.Ps. who wish to ask questions to submit them beforehand so that Ministers, who appear on a rota system, can prepare their replies. The system, which dates only from the end of the last century, is a splendid method for keeping Ministers on their toes, nagging at a problem and even extracting admissions embarrassing to the Ministers. The skill required is for the M.P. to ask a supplementary question to catch the Minister 'on the hop' after a bland response to the initial, prepared PQ.

   On the other hand, many critics have pointed out that the potential of the system is by no means fully exploited. There is just not enough time. The hour in practice shrinks to about 55 minutes; most questions cannot therefore be dealt with orally and have to be handled by written answers printed in *Hansard* (see p.13). Moreover, Governments have naturally not arranged for any extension of the time allocation and within the restrictions

Question Time

Ministers can often evade too much exposure—partly because the rota system makes any individual's appearance fairly infrequent (about monthly), and partly because of the delay between the sending in of a question and its appearance on the Order Paper.

Committees

As we have seen in Chapter 6 much detailed parliamentary work is undertaken in committee. Backbenchers and members of Opposition parties can exercise some leverage on the government in this context.

The power of M.Ps.

Lobby-fodder?

When the House of Commons evolved in the medieval and early modern periods of English history there were no political parties. During the past century or so party discipline has hardened to such an extent that many commentators (including some M.Ps. themselves) believe that the original idea of an M.P. as an independent-minded individual has been utterly lost. The 'Whips' ensure that the M.P.s of their party troop into the appropriate lobby to vote in divisions according to the 'party line'. And even without this organised discipline, M.Ps. who frequently speak or write against the policy of their leaders might be passed over for ministerial or shadow ministerial posts. Does this, then, mean that back-bench M.Ps. have no will or conscience of their own?

Opportunities for independence

In fact, many M.Ps. are not quite such robots. M.Ps. often oppose their party leaders; they can and do express their independent views at party conferences, in meetings of or dominated by backbenchers (e.g. the Conservative 1922 Committee, the Parliamentary Labour Party). Some are indeed quite famous for their opposition to their leaders—in recent years the 'far-left' in the Labour Party and the 'wets' in the Conservative. And increasingly Members on the Government back-benches have shown themselves willing to abstain or even vote against the Government on certain issues. In the last resort, M.Ps. can change parties, even start a new one, as in the case of the S.D.P.

8
Parliamentary debates

The importance of debates

Parliament is a 'talking-shop'. Parliament is a place where politicians can speak about public matters, express points of view, argue, try to persuade, support and oppose other members. Indeed, the very word tells us that this is its function (compare the French 'parler', to speak). What is more, this free exchange of ideas is vital for a democratic form of government. People are bound to differ about political and economic priorities; and wise and just policies are more likely to result from widespread discussion than from decisions made by a few.

Different types of debate

The rules of parliamentary procedure allow for different kinds of debates, which may be classified in different ways. The main occasions and types are as follows:

Adjournment

At the end of each day's business 30 minutes are allowed for debates initiated by M.Ps. chosen by ballot. This time is usually employed by M.Ps. to raise constituency matters for answer by a junior minister. The occasions are very useful for ventilating issues which might otherwise be ignored in the pressure of major business and legislation.

Queen's Speech

Each new session of Parliament is opened by a Speech from the Throne, in which the Government's programme for the year is outlined. During the following few days the House of Commons debates the contents of this speech. In this way the Government can judge the attitude of the House to its plans.

The Speech from the Throne

Government

Most formal speeches are those made on business initiated by the Government, as indeed is the debate on the Queen's Speech. All debates on Government-sponsored bills, for example, fall into this category. There are also, of course, debates on all specialist matters such as foreign policy, defence, the economy. Provision is also made for general Adjournment debates (not to be confused with the half-hour variety). These allow for wide-ranging debate on a chosen topic, but no decision is reached or resolution passed. All these debates are, typically, dominated by frontbench spokesmen, reading from prepared texts or notes and last several hours.

Opposition

Since 1985 the House has allotted twenty 'Opposition Days' (three for the second largest Opposition party—at present the Liberal Democrats) in the year. On each of these the Opposition selects its own topic, naturally choosing one which it thinks will most effectively embarrass the Government, and moves a motion; this is normally amended by a Government amendment after a division.

Censure

Occasionally the Opposition may raise a motion of censure to express its outrage at a Government action. The motion is debated before the vote is taken.

Backbenchers

Although in most general set-piece debates back-benchers enjoy some opportunity to contribute, they cannot choose the subject of these debates. However, nine Fridays and four half-Mondays in each year are allocated to private-members' motions when they can take the initiative. For this purpose M.Ps. are selected by ballot to table a motion and open the debate.

Emergency

Any M.P. may apply for the suspension of agreed business to debate a matter of pressing importance. The Speaker must rule whether the matter is covered by Standing Order Number 20 regulating emergency debates and the House must decide, if it does, whether to interrupt its business or not. Only about two or three applications a year are granted, although they are made almost daily.

House of Lords

Debates in the House of Lords have a slightly different character from those in the lower House. The peers usually draw upon a life-time of relevant experience in making their speeches. They are, moreover, less constrained than the Commons by shortage of time and strictness of Party discipline.

What makes a good Parliamentary orator?

Parliamentary debate requires two kinds of skills: the ability to engage in the cut-and-thrust of argument and to deliver a prepared speech. For argument the speaker needs specifically a good memory stored with relevant information in order to counter factual statements; speed of thought and fluency of speech quickly to marshal and express his reaction to the previous speaker. In addition, he needs the qualities which form the ingredients of a good prepared speech. For this purpose he must obviously have audible and clear diction, an interesting tone of voice, be sensitive to language in both the choice of words and the rhythm of sentences. He must be able to judge the mood of the House and adapt his wit or sombre style to match the occasion. He must never be dull and always have something of importance to say. Finally, a commanding presence and positive personality are crucial.

One M.P. who met most nearly all these criteria in this century was Winston Churchill. In praising his stature as an orator, A.P. Herbert wrote:

> The 'orator' is a person of power. He may appeal to a sense of logic ..., to a sense of justice, or duty, the sublime or the ridiculous. But one way or another, he stirs the hearts and minds

Not all debates are as well-attended as the one in this 1849 cartoon, nor are as many MPs as likely to doze off!

of men as he desires, commanding their deeds or endurance, their judgment or their money, their verdict or their vote... By any standard, by any definition, he is a great orator.

Another was 'Nye' Bevan. Both could turn an argument and make people see an old problem in a new way.

Is there room for improvement?

A proportion of the valuable time of the House of Commons is consumed by members delivering long, prepared speeches to a small audience. There is little incentive for M.Ps. to attend for most of these speeches. The Whips ensure that on almost every occasion the vote is a foregone conclusion however persuasive.

Should, then, 'speeches' not be circulated beforehand and the authors of the papers subjected to detailed questioning in the Chamber? More time for debate in this sense might be a more efficient use of parliamentary time.

9
The broadcasting of Parliament

The importance of broadcasting

Parliament is no longer a secret place. Newspapers have carried reports and *Hansard* has printed speeches for generations. Furthermore, members of the public are allowed into galleries to attend debates. What more natural, then, than to allow as many people as wish to listen to or watch debates through the media of radio and television? And yet the broadcasting of Parliament has been a controversial matter.

The House of Lords in session. The introduction of TV cameras has had little effect.

Sound broadcasting

Origins

One of the keenest Ministers to advocate the reform of Parliament in recent years was R.H.S. Crossman, who was the Leader of the House of Commons 1967–68. In his *Diaries* he described his attitude to broadcasting:

> *Tuesday, April 30th 1968*
> A little box has been built in at the back where the officials sit and here we have a man from the B.B.C. and one of our door keepers to tell him the names of the people who are up. The B.B.C. are now experimenting with half-hour and quarter-hour programmes using the actual words of M.Ps.... Of all the reforms I've introduced this is the one I'd like to see pushed through, since it would change the House more than anything else if people outside could hear the misbehaviour which now goes on.

However, another ten years were to pass before sound broadcasts from the House of Commons were made regular. And sadly Crossman's hopes of their improving behaviour have not been fulfilled.

The present system

Since 1978 the proceedings of both Houses have been broadcast. These sound recordings are used, for example, by B.B.C. Radio 4 for its morning programme 'Yesterday in Parliament' and late-night programme 'Today in Parliament'. Most people, however, hear the voices of ministers and M.Ps. in the context of television news bulletins, in which snippets of debates are used over still pictures to convey the main thrust of arguments concerning a newsworthy issue.

Television

The House of Lords

As early as 1966 the House of Lords voted in favour of the principle that its proceedings should be televised. But it was not until January 1985 that the first live television transmission was made.

Both B.B.C. and I.T.N. videotape the proceedings they think will be of interest and use the material in a variety of ways; for example, in news bulletins, current affairs programmes, nightly or weekly summaries of the Lords' business and occasionally special programmes. The effects of television, like sound broadcasting, have not been as far-reaching as many people expected: after the novelty had worn off, it neither stimulated public interest in the House of Lords to any great extent; nor were their Lordships excessively conscious of being 'on camera'.

The House of Commons

And yet the Commons still hesitated. Many M.Ps. remained nervous that the average citizen would be disillusioned with his representatives if he witnessed on his screen a pathetically sparse and sleepy attendance, or M.Ps. in excitable and rowdy mood. But this is largely an editorial question: with limited air time at their disposal can the broadcasters be trusted to present a balanced impression of parliamentary business? Despite these hesitations, in 1988 the House voted in favour of arranging an experimental period of television broadcasting to test its acceptability.

Not everyone was in favour of televising the Commons!

10
The Lobby correspondent

What is 'the Lobby'?

Origins

The need for security against terrorists, so evident to the visitor to the Palace of Westminster today, is not new. Until just over a hundred years ago, the Member's Lobby outside the Chamber of the House of Commons was accessible to the public and journalists also. The fear of Fenian (Irish) bombings forced its closure to all outsiders except a limited number of the press. It is this privileged group of political correspondents, who by the end of the last century had also established an office at 10 Downing Street, that came to be called 'the Lobby'.

The Lobby today

Members of the Lobby are those newspaper, radio and television journalists who wish to be members and who have been accepted as professionally worthy. The official list, nearly 150 today, is kept by the Serjeant at Arms. The Lobby has some kind of corporate existence: a chairman and committee and a list of rules. These rules concentrate on the responsibility of members to ensure the confidentiality of their briefings. For the main purpose of the Lobby is to enable the Prime Minister, other ministers and M.Ps. to supply information without revealing the exact nature of its source. The rules therefore assert that 'The cardinal rule of the Lobby is never to identify its informant without specific permission' and *don't talk about Lobby meetings before or after they are held.*

A democratic system of government cannot be sustained unless the public is informed about policies and events. In Britain much of the political information presented by the media is channelled through the Lobby. Is this a good system?

Advantages of the system

The Lobby has a strict code of conduct and members may be expelled if they breach the rules. Ministers and M.Ps. therefore feel that they can trust these journalists to use the information they are given with discretion. Members of the Lobby are consequently supplied with information which otherwise would not be divulged or would not be released so soon. The Lobby journalists can write with this background information in mind. They are also assured of a regular flow of material to pass on to the public. Most politicians and journalists feel that the system works well.

Disadvantages of the system

Nevertheless, in recent years particularly, a number of criticisms have been levelled at the arrangement. Indeed, since 1986 neither *The Independent* nor *The Guardian* correspondents have been members of the Lobby, and the system has as a result been weakened.

The main objection is that the Lobby is presented with information which the politicians wish to see printed. Therefore, it is alleged, political correspondents do not seek out other sources of news with sufficient zeal and the investigative vigour of the news media is undermined. As a consequence the public sometimes reads a partial and therefore biased story. Two features of the system have been particular sources of criticism. One is the close relationship of the prime minister's Press Officer and the Lobby. The other is the practice of non-attributable mass-briefings. All correspondents are in this way given the same pre-digested material and yet are forbidden to reveal the identity of their informant.

Lawson accuses press of ———— misunderstandings and ———— a 'farrago of invention'

By Peter Pryke
Parliamentary Correspondent

Mr Lawson, Chancellor of the Exchequer, denied amid angry scenes in the Commons yesterday that his weekend press briefing had revealed his intentions to impose means tests for retirement pensions, the £10 Christmas bonus, or free health prescriptions for pensioners.

Instead he accused the journalists who attended his Friday briefing of having produced "a farrago of invention."

"They know they went behind afterwards, and they thought they did not have a good enough story—and so

they produced that which bore no relation what-ever to what I have said," he said.

Labour received Mr Lawson's explanation with total scepticism, and the SPEAKER, Mr Weatherill, had to invervene on several occasions, first to appeal for a fair hearing for Mr Kinnock and then for the Chancellor.

The belief that Mr Lawson had let slip the Tories' "hidden agenda" for cutting back the welfare state excited Labour MPs, and there was a sharp exchange when Mr FRANK FIELD, a Labour expert in the field, proclaimed Mr Lawson's "gaffe" as a Labour election winner.

A senior Tory and former minister, Sir ANTHONY GRANT (Cambridgeshire SW) asked: "In view of the dangers of misreporting, would it not be a good idea to refrain from gabbing to the press until the policies are clear?"

Mr LAWSON replied that as a former minister, Sir Anthony would recall that it was customary for ministers to talk to the press on an off-the-record basis from time to time.

Mr ALAN BEITH (Dem, Berwick-upon-Tweed) asked how the Chancellor, a former journalist, could have managed to mislead so many journalists at once.

An extract from *The Daily Telegraph* of 8 November 1988.
A row had blown up between the Chancellor of the Exchequer, Nigel Lawson, and the Lobby. Lawson claimed that off-the-record remarks he had made had not only been 'leaked', but leaked inaccurately. The Lobby claimed otherwise.

11
A Golden Age of Parliament?

The decline of Parliament?

Loss of reputation

What's Wrong With Parliament? was the title of one of several books published in the late 1950s and early 1960s which bewailed the decline in the quality and effectiveness of the work of Parliament, and particularly the House of Commons. The general attitude was summed up in the following way in this book: 'In 1945 the reputation of the British Parliament stood as high as ever before in its long history ....[But] A notable leader in *The Times* on 23 October 1957 said that the House of Commons contained "far too many little men", engaged in "desperate fighting over things that do not matter".' And the public has shown its scorn for this second-rate institution, so it was argued, by losing interest. If this is true and if public apathy concerning parliamentary affairs has continued, the matter may be cause for some concern: after all, is not a vigorous parliament essential for the sustenance of democracy?

Strength of the executive

In particular, Parliament should be restraining the Executive branch of government from becoming too powerful. Yet there are signs that it is becoming increasingly strong. This is partly because the Government can normally expect to command an automatic majority in the Commons. Moreover, there has also been a strengthening of the position of the prime minister. Already in the

1960s there was a speculation about whether Harold Wilson was developing a 'presidential' style of government. In the 1980s the comments have concerned Mrs Thatcher's authoritarian style of government. Indeed, so secure has Mrs Thatcher's majority in the Commons been that some Labour M.Ps. came to feel at times that attendance was futile. Thus the Opposition has sometimes so obviously failed to oppose successfully that the House of Lords (aided by some Government back-benchers) has become in the view of some politicians a more effective check on government.

A unique development

In 1865 John Bright described England as 'the mother of Parliaments'. Until the late eighteenth century no other country had succeeded in developing such an institution; indeed, many looked to England to learn and, to a certain extent, to copy.

The fame of the English parliament lay particularly in its resistance to the monarchy in the century from the 1580s to 1680s. In the later years of Elizabeth I and in the reigns of Charles I and James II Parliament, when convened, voiced its hostility to what M.Ps. considered the dangers of excessive royal power. In the 1640s this hostility led even to civil war and the execution of the king.

In the nineteenth century Parliament reached maturity with the huge increase in reforming legislation and the fine oratorical skills of many politicians, most famously of those arch-rivals Gladstone and Disraeli.

The problem of comparisons

When people refer to 'the Golden Age of Parliament' they usually mean the period c.1832–1880. But historical comparisons can be dangerous. This is partly because of man's somehow natural habit to complain about the present and to view the past through nostalgia-tinted memory.

Partly, too, we must always guard against the assumption that criteria of judgment can remain constant. Parliament today cannot exhibit the same qualities as Parliament of yesteryear (whenever that was) because the nature of government is different. The two World Wars of this century forced a great expansion of the machinery of central government and the complexities of the ensuing peace-time years, notably the issues of the economy and defence, have made it very difficult for that machinery to be dismantled. Mrs Thatcher, who started famously bent upon reducing central government interference has notoriously come to increase that tendency, for example, by reducing the authority of local government and emphasising the need for secrecy.

The question is therefore not so much, Has Parliament declined in prestige and power? It is, rather, How can Parliament be most effectively reformed to discharge its essential democratic functions in the political world of the late twentieth century?

Perhaps things haven't changed so much, after all!

12
The reform of Parliament

The problem

Adaptability

Parliament has survived in England for something like seven centuries because it has been constantly adapted to cope with changing circumstances over the ages. The membership has altered; the organisation of its business has altered; its powers and functions have altered; and the relationship between Lords and Commons has altered.

Today's challenge

There is no reason to believe that this process of change should come to a halt today. Indeed, society and government have become so complicated in recent decades that many critics feel Parliament has not adapted quickly enough to the demands of the twentieth century. Government now has enormous powers to control the economy, spend large sums of money and organise the armed forces. All these activities involve technical understanding and yet affect every citizen. Are our parliamentarians sufficiently equipped and capable of looking after the interests of the nation as effectively as possible?

The House of Lords

An anomaly?

Most larger countries recognise that it is useful to have a bicameral legislature—in British terms, two Houses of Parliament. Each chamber can share the work-load and give 'a second opinion' about the decisions of the other.

However, the House of Lords is a strange body. Its membership is a peculiar mixture of bishops, judges, life peers and hereditary peers. Only a small proportion of its members in practice attend. And because it is so obviously not representative of the nation, over the years it has been stripped of most of its former powers.

Possible changes

There are two main arguments for change. One is the radical case that a group of privileged people should have no constitutional part to play in a democratic state like Britain: the House of Lords should be abolished. The second is the moderate case that if a second chamber is useful, Britain should have one that is properly selected (e.g. to represent the different U.K. regions) and with enhanced functions and powers.

Nevertheless, no one has been able to devise an acceptable alternative. The invention of life peerages in 1958 merely tinkered with the problem, though it helped to revive the Lords. Moreover, during Mrs Thatcher's administrations since 1979 the left-wing have been manoeuvred into the embarrassing irony of seeing the 'privileged' House of Lords acting as a more effective check on the Conservative Government than the Labour Opposition in the Commons!

This cartoon is nearly thirty years old. In the 1980s, however, the Lords helped to act as a check to a government with a large majority

The House of Commons

Weaknesses

We saw in the last chapter how some politicians and political scientists have noticed a decline in the respect accorded by the public to Parliament. More recently, some have argued that there must surely be some connexion between Britain's economic decline and the lack of democracy in her political system; and that a reform of Parliament is the essential corrective. For example, in 1987 Professor Ridley analysed the most recent election results in the seventeen European countries with parliamentary systems to discover what percentage of voters supported the party or parties which them formed the government. He showed that Switzerland was the most 'democratic' by this test, because 77.5% voted for the government. Britain was bottom of the list, with only 42.3% voting Conservative in the election of that year. And in Parliament the Conservatives had a majority over all other parties of 101.

A breakdown of the time spent in Parliament on different kinds of business

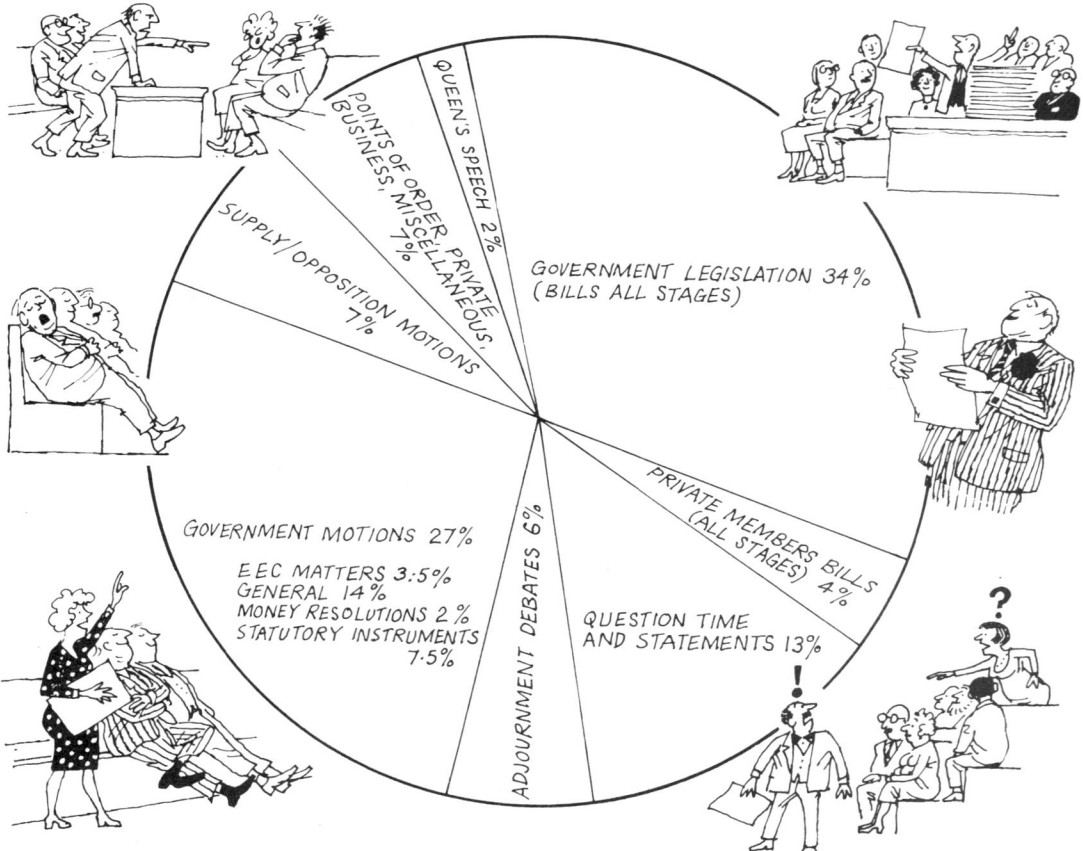

QUEEN'S SPEECH 2%

POINTS OF ORDER, PRIVATE BUSINESS, MISCELLANEOUS. 7%

SUPPLY/OPPOSITION MOTIONS. 7%

GOVERNMENT LEGISLATION 34%
(BILLS ALL STAGES)

GOVERNMENT MOTIONS 27%
EEC MATTERS 3.5%
GENERAL 14%
MONEY RESOLUTIONS 2%
STATUTORY INSTRUMENTS
7.5%

ADJOURNMENT DEBATES 6%

PRIVATE MEMBERS BILLS
(ALL STAGES) 4%

QUESTION TIME
AND STATEMENTS 13%

Procedural changes

Many advocates of parliamentary reform since the 1950s have argued that the conduct of business in the House of Commons should be updated and reformed. Some reforms have been introduced over the past quarter-of-a-century, most notably the Select Committee system (see Chapter 6). These reforms seem not to have made a great deal of difference. Consequently schemes for strengthening the powers of the committees or for encouraging much greater independence of mind and action among M.Ps. have been canvassed.

Changes in composition

Other would-be reformers believe that changes in the conduct of Commons business have been tried and found wanting and that the Whips' control over most of their party is bound to inhibit the independence of M.Ps. These commentators put their faith in changing the membership of the House by changing the electoral system. A change to a system of proportional representation, they argue, would have two beneficial effects on the House of Commons. In the first place, by definition, the proportion of M.Ps. of each party would much more closely match the total number of votes cast for each party nationally. The House would therefore accurately reflect the political wishes of the total body of citizens. Secondly, such an arrangement would be most unlikely to produce a government with an unchallengeable majority in the Commons. Parliament would therefore have more power than at present vis-a-vis the Government.

Voting patterns in the 1983 election, by occupation

Class	Percentage voting			
	Conservative	Labour	Alliance	Other
Self-employed	71	12	17	0
Salaried and professional	54	14	31	1
Routine non-manual	46	25	27	2
Foremen and technicians	48	26	25	1
Working Class	30	49	20	1

Source: Heath, Jowell and Curtice (1985)

43

Which changes do you think would be most beneficial? To clarify your ideas you could draw out the table on page 44 and tick the boxes to indicate your views. For example, if you think the introduction of a proportional electoral system is important to render the Commons more representative, then tick that box. Then consider what the complications would be, if any, for the other boxes.

	Member-ship	Organisation of business	Powers and functions	Relationship between Lords and Commons
Legitimising*				
Representative				
Taxation and expenditure				
Redressing of grievances				
Legislature				
Recruiting of ministers				
Scrutinising and informing				
Judicial***				

 * Giving the government proper authority to govern
** House of Lords only

The ideal is probably a strong Government for firm leadership of the country and a strong Opposition in Parliament to prevent the abuse of that strength. The trick is to arrange a parliamentary system to achieve this fine balance.

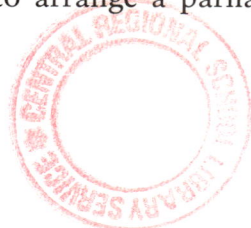

44